DYNAMIQUE

Oral revision for GCSE French

Ernesto Macaro

Edward Arnold

A division of Hodder & Stoughton

LONDON   BALTIMORE   MELBOURNE   AUCKLAND

ACKNOWLEDGMENTS

My thanks to all those teachers who participated in the Warwickshire Modern Language Workshops. Special thanks to Anne-Marie Gratacap for her help and advice.

EAM

British Library Cataloguing in Publication Data

Macaro, E.A.
   Dynamique.
   1. Spoken French language —— For schools
   I. Title
   448.3'421

First published 1988

ISBN 0–7131–7773X

Typeset in Linotron Univers and Plantin by Gecko Ltd, Bicester, Oxon
Printed in Great Britain for Edward Arnold, a division of Hodder and Stoughton Ltd, Mill Road, Dunton Green, Sevenoaks, Kent, by Richard Clay Ltd, Bungay, Suffolk

CONTENTS

Teacher's notes

The Student Cassette has been designed for use by the student prior to GCSE oral examination. Primarily it is a means of revising, at home, a variety of topics and a series of language structures. However the dialogues can also be used in the language laboratory or with individual audio recorders throughout the two years leading up to the examination. The underlying intention is to encourage student-orientated learning whereby he/she can carry out a variety of tasks at his/her own speed and with minimal help from the teacher.

This Student's Book has also been devised to help the student work on his/her own. It contains diagrams showing how each of the tasks in the role play situations falls into a language function and it gives the student some useful hints on how to approach the oral exam. We have, therefore, used mainly instructions such as 'tell', 'express', 'enquire', 'ask', rather than simply 'say', to encourage the student to think about what effect the language he/she is going to use is meant to produce. Moreover it is hoped that this will also encourage the student to use his/her own knowledge of French to find a way round a problem.

The role-play dialogues have been arranged in six topic groups, within which certain dialogues are marked with an asterisk to indicate that they are intended for higher level students only. The topics are:

1 Travel	Basic: 1, 2	Higher:	3, 4, 5, 6
2 Preparations for a holiday	Basic: 7, 8, 9	Higher:	10, 11
3 Campsite	Basic: 12, 13	Higher:	14, 15, 16, 17
4 Leisure activities	Basic: 18, 19	Higher:	20, 21, 22
5 Talking to strangers	Basic: 23	Higher:	24, 25
6 Talking to friends	Basic: 26, 27	Higher:	28, 29, 30

How the student's book might be used

As there are English prompts on the Student Cassette, the student can revise at home without further assistance from the teacher. However, teachers may wish to prepare their students in class by working through the role-play situations with them: explaining structures and revising vocabulary. This can either be done by asking them all to practise a single situation at a time or by different pairs of students working on different situations within a topic. Before starting to practise the role play situations in pairs, teachers may wish to let the students hear the dialogues on the cassette. After listening to the relevant dialogues, the students should calmly study the tasks required of them. They should try to work out which language function each of the tasks falls into (see *Student's notes*) and, if necessary, look at the reverse side of the page for the structures or the vocabulary that will help them. The French phrases have been set out at random so that what is required of the student is not a mechanical reading of sentences but a considerable effort of comprehension. During this time the teacher might need to give some assistance to those who are struggling. Then the pair-work can begin. When the teacher judges that the students have had sufficient time, he/she might ask a pair to perform the role-play while the rest of the class takes brief notes in the same way as they would during a listening comprehension exercise.

If you are using this cassette as a means of revision for your oral examination, here are some points that might be worth remembering.

A   Which 'language function'?

The things you're going to need to say – the language tasks – can be divided up into a number of categories (language functions). This is because language is like a tool which helps you to achieve something, usually for your own benefit. Try to memorize which bits of language (language structures) fit into which category. This will help you to sort out what is being asked of you during those precious minutes of preparation time.

Here are the categories:

1   Wanting   All the language bits in this circle can be used when you want the person with whom you are talking, to satisfy a material need (to get you something you want). Sometimes, the phrases look as if they're asking for information (e.g. *'est-ce qu'on peut acheter un plan ici?'*) but really they're asking for action! After all, you wouldn't be very satisfied if the person answered *'Oui'* and then walked away!

2   Enquiring   All the language bits in this circle can be used when you need any information about the world around you. Generally speaking the person you are talking to should answer with words not with actions. You'd think it a bit rude if at the Bureau de Renseignements you asked *'A quelle heure part le prochain train pour Metz?'* and without a word the employee handed you a thick, incomprehensible timetable book!

3   Greeting and getting along with others   All the language bits in this circle can be used when you want someone to be aware of your presence or when you are trying to set up a relationship of some sort. On your exam paper, tasks like these might not seem very important, but they are. Don't forget to include them! They're communicating something to the person who is listening just as much as the other tasks.

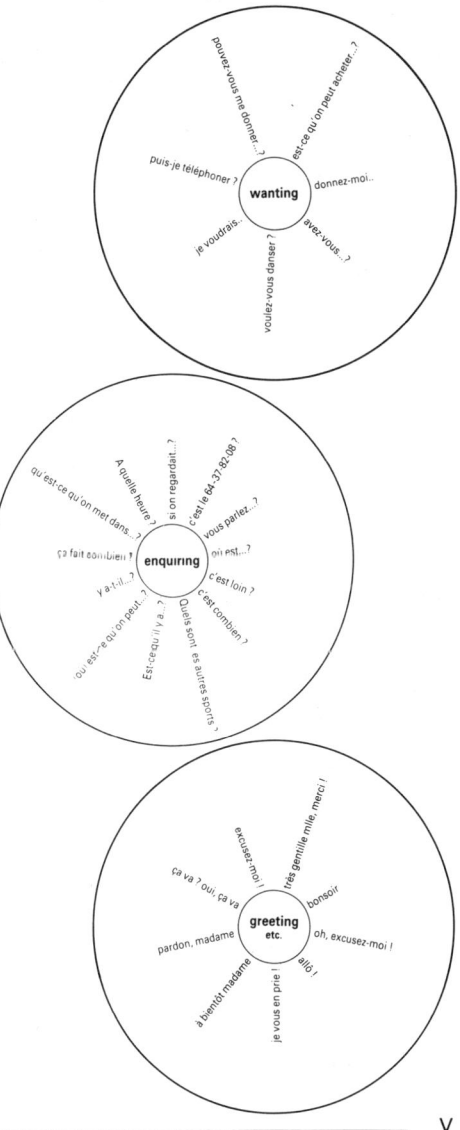

4 Stating Lots of language bits fall into this category. Basically, it's when you are giving someone information. Almost always, it's new information. The less the hearer expects what you're going to say, the more interesting it is for him/her.

5 Regulating All the language bits in this circle can be used when you want to control the behaviour of others. You're telling them or commanding them to do something. Of course, sometimes you have to do this as politely as possible!

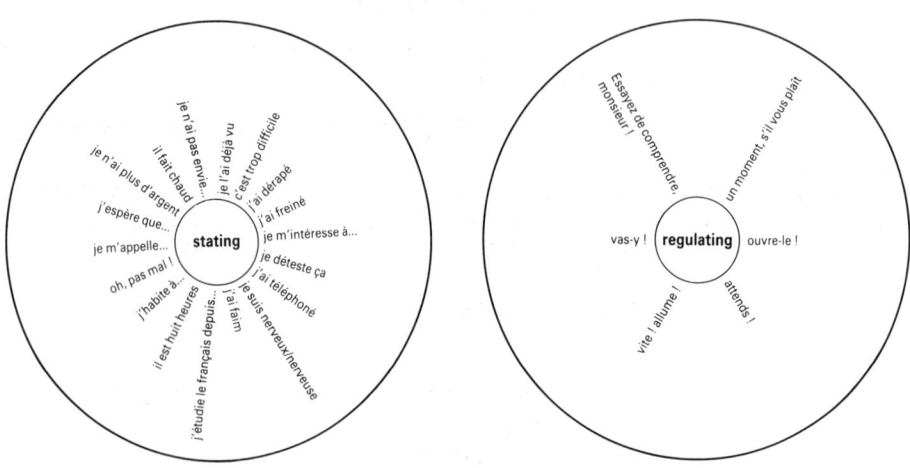

B Tone of voice
Remember too that the tone of your voice is very important. Questions go up at the end ⤴, statements go down ⤵. Let's take an example. The task is: 'ask how much that comes to'. However you can only remember the word 'combien'. As long as you say it with a very definite ⤴, you'll get *some* marks for it.

C Context
Always make sure you take into account the context or "setting" of the dialogues. Is it a formal setting? Will you need to use *vous* rather than *tu*? Are there any special conventions or 'ways of doing things', such as the way you make a phone call or answer a phone call in France? Is there any way that the context can help you get round a language problem?

D Working with the cassette
On the cassette there is a three second gap for each of your tasks. This is obviously not long enough for your response, so you will need to use the pause button. Always check that the French you have spoken is as close as possible in *pronunciation* to the 'native speaker' version that follows it.

Before starting to work on the tape, look through the role play tasks. Find any language bits you're not sure of by consulting the 'functions' circles. Good luck!

TOPIC 1 Travel

RP 1a	You are phoning a French family (la famille Didot) to give them details of your arrival. Your name is Louise Townsend. You recognise that it's Mme. Didot who has picked up the phone.

    a   Greet her and ask if that is number 12–48–38–85.

    b   Tell her who you are.

    c   You are well. Enquire how she is.

    d   Tell her that you are arriving on 15th June at 3pm (use 24 hour clock) at the Gare du Nord.

    e   Thank her. Tell her you'll see her soon, then say goodbye.

RP 2a	You are travelling with a French friend who is very worried that you may have left something behind. You are standing on the platform waiting for the train. He/she speaks first.

    a   Yes, they're in your bag.

    b   It's there, on the seat!

    c   Tell him/her that it's over there, by the wall. Say that he/she is very edgy today!
Ask where his/her passport is.

*RP 3a	At Orleans station you meet an Englishman who needs your help:
	    he can't speak French;
	    he is going to La Rochelle;
	    he has missed his connection.

Go to the information desk and make enquiries on his behalf.

    a   Tell the employee what's happened. Then ask the time of the next train for La Rochelle (take notes for him).

    b   Show concern! Ask if he will have to change.

    c   Ask from which platform it leaves.

    d   Ask what time it arrives in La Rochelle.

    e   Ask if there is a hotel nearby. A cheap one!

    f   Thank the assistant.

1a

c'est le . . .	use *aller* to describe how you are (*ça va bien!*)
	allô
et vous?	à bientôt Madame

2a

où est ton passeport?

le/la/les voilà!   dans mon sac

que tu es nerveux/nerveuse aujourd'hui!

sur le siège   contre le mur

*3a

c'est/à quelle heure?   le prochain train

ce monsieur ne parle pas français!

. . . raté sa correspondance

oh mon Dieu!!   en retard
pas trop cher!

Est-ce qu'il y a . . .?

quel quai s'il vous plaît?

pas trop cher!   c'est direct?
                                                       il doit changer?
près d'ici

*RP 4a — You've missed your connection to Marseille. You need to phone the people you'll be staying with so you go to the buffet de gare.

a   Ask the man at the counter if you can make a phone call.

b   Thank him then ask for the code for Marseille.

c   Oh yes; you had forgotten.

d   Dial the number. Ask if that's 51–34–45–67?

e   Say who you are and that you're still in Lyon.

f   Ask her to repeat it. You haven't understood.

g   Say yes. You missed the connection. You'll arrive at 18.35.

h   Say: yes, see you later. Goodbye.

*RP5 — You are on a train travelling from Lille to Calais. The *contrôleur* comes up to you. You search for your ticket and you start getting that sinking feeling!

a   Tell him you think it's in your bag. There it is! Then: no, that's a luggage ticket.

b   (You try again) You've got it! No, no. That's a metro ticket.

c   Admit to him that you can't find your ticket.

d   Act offended! Say: of course, you've lost it that's all!

e   Tell him you bought it in Lille.

f   28 Francs, you think.

g   No, a single.

h   Plead with him! Tell him: that's impossible. Ask him to be reasonable (don't forget to say Monsieur, it might help!).

*RP 6a — You have finally arrived at your French destination and you are met by your host family. Naturally they will want to know what sort of journey you've had. Your partner speaks first.

a   Tell him/her that it wasn't a bad journey, a bit tiring.

b   This morning you left at about 8 o'clock.

c   Yes, the sea was fairly calm.

d   That's right, you had to wait 40 minutes for the connection.

e   You bought a sandwich from the station buffet.

f   You talked to a French boy on the train. You read a magazine.

*4a

on peut téléphoner d'ici?   j'avais oublié

je suis toujours à . . .

l'indicatif

je n'ai pas compris   j'ai raté la . . .

à tout à l'heure

*5a

je crois
bien sûr!

le/la/les voilà!   un ticket de consigne

je l'ai perdu, voilà tout!
je l'ai acheté à Lille

je ne trouve pas . . .   un aller simple

mais ce n'est pas possible!   essayez de comprendre,
monsieur!

*6a

(Apart from **a** and **c**, you are
basically telling a story in the
past tense: you need **two**
oh, pas mal   **words** for the verb!)

je suis parti(e)   pour la correspondance

j'ai dû attendre   j'ai lu . . .   un peu fatigant
j'ai acheté . . .
j'ai bavardé avec . . .   . . . était assez calme

TOPIC 2 Preparations for a holiday

RP 7a You are off on holiday with your French family. However you must first stop to fill up with petrol. Your hosts insist that you ask for it.

    a   Ask the attendant for 25 litres of four-star petrol.

    b   Ask him to check the tyres and the oil.

    c   Ask if you can buy a map at the garage.

    d   Say thank you and goodbye.

RP 8a You have decided to go to the camping shop to buy equipment for the holiday. You have been told what is needed and you have jotted these down:

sleeping bag (must be blue or green)
2 tea towels
bottle gas
folding chair
torch (must not cost more than 60F)
cheap two-man tent (must not cost more than 300F)
small rucksack (must not cost more than 180F)

Ask the assistant for the things on your list. Make a note of the things you actually buy.

RP 9a You go shopping for the food. You can't drive to the supermarket so you go down to the local épicerie.

    a   Greet the shopkeeper (a young girl).

    b   Ask for eight bottles of mineral water and four bottles of red wine.

    c   Ask for some cheese (a creamy one and a blue cheese).

    d   You want 400g of pate, and some coffee.

    e   You want ground coffee.

    f   You also want some drinking chocolate.

    g   Ask how much it comes to.

    h   Say thank you and goodbye.

7a

les pneus
une carte   l'huile   . . . de super s'il vous plaît

  voulez-vous vérifier . . . ?

Est-ce qu'on peut
acheter . . .

8a

Avez-vous . . . ?

Alors, je voudrais . . .

sac de couchage

torchon   bouteille de gaz

torche

tente (canadienne)
sac à dos
chaise pliante

pas trop chèr(e)
non, c'est trop cher
quelque chose de . . . ?

ça fait combien?

9a

Je voudrais . . .
. . . d'eau minérale
ça fait combien?   . . . de vin rouge
du chocolat en poudre

du café
Camembert   du pâté
. . . oeufs
Bleu de Bresse

moulu s'il vous plaît

TOPIC 2 Preparations for a holiday

*RP 10a	You are helping your French friend load the family car for the camping holiday. You suggest to one another where various items should go. You start first.

   a Ask what you should put in the boot.

   b There isn't enough room for the water carrier. Suggest putting it under the back seat.

   c Yes, that's fine. Ask where you should put the tin opener.

   d That's OK. Ask where the rope should go.

   e Ask if that's all.

*RP 11a	You are about to go on a camping holiday with a French family. Your partner is trying to get you to help him/her.

You'd like to: do the shopping
see to the car
check the camping equipment
look after the animals

You wouldn't like to: tidy the house
do the housework
do the washing
do the ironing

There are still things to do. Offer to get the suitcases and make the coffee.

*10a

c'est tout?

Qu'est-ce qu'on met
dans . . . ?
où est-ce qu'on met . . . ?
si on le mettait sous . . . ?

le siège   le coffre   la corde

ça va!

il n'y a pas assez de . . .

arrière/à l'avant   l'ouvre-boîtes

le bidon

*11a

faire les courses
m'occuper des animaux
m'occuper de la voiture
vérifier les équipements de
camping

oui, je veux bien . . .
non, je n'aime pas . . .   est-ce que je peux?
je préfère   prendre les valises
                                    préparer le café

TOPIC 3 Campsite

RP 12a You have arrived at a campsite.

a Greet the male warden. Ask if he has any room.

b Tell him it's for one tent.

c It's for only one night and for two people.

d Say: yes, certainly. Then thank him.

RP 13a You have arrived at a campsite.

a Greet the warden, a young lady.

b Ask if she has any room. It is for a family of six with two tents.

c It's for four days, until 14th August.

d Thank the warden then say: It's hot today!

*RP 14a Your name is Louise Townsend and you are on a cycling holiday, in Bourgogne, with a friend. Understandably, you don't want to arrive at your next campsite only to find it full. Make a phone call:

a When someone answers ask if that's 84–37–82–08.

b Ask if it is the Mogador campsite.

c You'd like to book a place for the day after tomorrow. That's the 26th July.

d It's a tent, a small one.

e You're on bikes. Two adults.

f One night only.

g Say yes, then tell the person your name.

h Spell Townsend (French alphabet!). Tell him/her that's your surname.

i Say thank you and goodbye.

12a

c'est pour . . .

Oui, bien sûr

une nuit
une tente
deux personnes

avez-vous de la place s'il vous plaît

13a

avez-vous . . . ?
c'est pour . . .
avec . . .

une famille de six
. . . de la place?

jusqu'au

il fait . . . !

*14a

c'est le . . . ?

je voudrais réserver un emplacement pour le . . .

nous sommes . . .

ça c'est mon nom de famille . . .
. . . deux adultes

à vélo
une nuit seulement

TOPIC 3 Campsite

*RP 15a
You have arrived at a campsite. You know there shouldn't be any problem because you phoned yesterday. But you never know!

a   Greet the warden. Tell her you booked in the name of Thompson.

b   No, you phoned yesterday.

c   Say: yes that's right.

d   Say: yes, of course. Ask what the price is.

e   Ask if there is a restaurant. Tell her that you are very tired and you don't want to cook this evening.

f   Thank her and say: good evening!

*RP 16a
You have arrived at a campsite after a hard day's drive. You're looking forward to a shower and a meal.

a   Greet the male warden and ask if he has room for a caravan.

b   Express annoyance. Ask if there is another campsite nearby.

c   Ask if it is a comfortable campsite. Tell him you've done a lot of miles today.

d   Ask him if he can give you the phone number (write it down).

e   Ask if you can phone from the campsite. You'll pay, of course.

f   Thank the warden.

*RP 17a
You are staying on a French campsite. Whilst heating up some tinned Cassoulet for your lunch you are approached by a young Frenchman who is carrying out a survey on camping in France. He will ask you some questions. To these you reply the following:

a   Your name is Jane/Alan Robertson. (You'll have to spell it!)

b   You are from Glasgow in Scotland.

c   This is your first time in France.

d   You have two weeks holiday.

e   You are staying on this campsite for three days.

f   You are with a group of friends.

g   You have a small tent.

(What's he saying about your Cassoulet???) React in French!

*15a

j'ai fait une réservation
. . . j'ai téléphoné . . .

au nom de . . .   ça fait . . . ?

bonsoir!

oui, c'est ça   Est-ce qu'il y a . . . ?
oui, bien sûr!   cuisiner
je n'ai pas envie de . . .
je suis très fatigué

*16a

Oh zut!

. . . de la place?   j'ai fait pas mal de
                                                    kilomètres . . .
y a-t-il un autre
camping . . . ?   pouvez-vous me donner
c'est un camping . . . ?   le . . .

je payerai . . .   puis-je téléphoner . . .
. . . tout confort?   . . . près d'ici

*17a

je m'appelle . . .   j'ai une petite . . .
                                               j'ai deux . . .

                je suis de . . . en . . .
                je suis avec . . .

je reste ici pour . . .   c'est ma première fois . . .

| **RP 18a** | You are at a tourist office. |

a   Greet the receptionist.

b   You want a map of the region.

c   You would also like a leaflet about the town.

d   Ask what time the museum opens.

e   Say thank you and goodbye.

| **RP 19a** | You go to a French tourist office. You've had enough of culture. Now, how about some fun! |

a   Greet the receptionist.

b   Ask if there is a disco in town.

c   Ask where the cinema is.

d   Ask if it is open every evening.

e   Thank her.

| ***RP 20a** | You are at the entrance to the campsite where you have been staying for a few days. A French person who has just arrived starts asking you some questions. He/she speaks first. This is what you tell him/her about the place. |

a   You've been there for three days.

b   It's a good campsite. Pleasant. You like it.

c   There's a swimming pool and a games room.

d   There is a lake 500 metres away. You can fish, go sailing and canoeing.

e   Finally say: you're welcome!

18a

Avez-vous . . . ?
Je voudrais aussi . . .
A quelle heure ouvre . . . ?

un dépliant sur la ville
une carte de la région
le musée

19a

Où est . . . ?
Est-ce qu'il y a . . . ?

une discothèque
. . . tous les soirs?

c'est ouvert . . . ?

*20a

je vous en prie!

c'est très bien/c'est très
agréable
il y a une . . . et une salle de
jeux
. . . le lac à . . .
faire de la voile
faire du canoë

je suis là depuis . . .
on peut . . .
pêcher

TOPIC 4 Leisure activities

*RP 21a

You go to the tourist information office because you want to plan the next four days of your holiday. Today is Monday 13th June. The receptionist is going to give you quite a lot of information, so jot it down.

  a Greet the receptionist.

  b Tell her that you're interested in water skiing. Can you do this at the lake?

  c Ask if you can hire the equipment there.

  d You've also heard about an antiques shop in Brassy.

  e Ask if it's interesting.

  f Check the date of the exhibition (13th – 18th June).

  g Ask for the opening hours of the swimming pool in Luzy.

  h Say: You've been very kind, thank you, goodbye.

*RP 22a

It's your last few days in Bourgogne so you want to make the most of them. Perhaps some more sport. Oh yes, there's the disco tomorrow and camping hasn't done much for your hair style! You go to the tourist information office again. Take notes!

  a Greet the receptionist. He/she recognises you.

  b Tell him/her you enjoyed it. It's difficult though! Ask what other sports you can do in the area.

  c Tell him/her you'd like that. You've done that in England.

  d Say: thank you, good idea, then ask where you can play French bowls.

  e Say: a little. Is it far?

  f You agree to go. Now ask if there is a cheap hairdresser's in town.

  g Thank him/her and say goodbye.

*21a

j'ai entendu parler d' . . .
est-ce qu'on peut en faire sur
le lac?
. . . y louer l'équipement?

je suis un(e) passionné(e)   . . . un magasin d'antiquités
du ski nautique
c'est intéressant?

quelles sont les heures
d'ouvertures de . . . ?
            vous avez été très
aimable . . .

            du 13 juin jusqu'au . . . ?

*22a

            Où est-ce qu'on peut . . . ?

c'est loin?   oui, je me suis beaucoup
c'est difficile!   amusé(e)
                    j'en ai fait en . . .
            oui, j'aimerais bien faire . . .

Quels sont les autres
sports qu'on peut . . .
Est-ce qu' . . . un coiffeur
pas trop cher . . .

jouer à la pétanque   un peu
                    bonne idée!

RP 23a

You are travelling by train through France. A French person on the train asks where you are from. (He/she speaks first).

a   Tell him/her you're English (Welsh etc.). Introduce yourself.

b   You are going to Lyon.

c   Tell him/her where in England (Wales/Scotland etc.) you live.

d   Tell him/her how old you are.

e   Ask if he/she speaks English.

f   Say: thank you.

*RP 24a

You are on the sideline watching a friendly football match between some French and English youngsters. The second half has just started. A Frenchman asks you what you think of the match. (He speaks first.)

a   You think it's a good match. It was an interesting first half.

b   Perhaps because the French are younger.

c   You agree. There haven't been many fouls.

d   The French team is trying to equalise, though.

e   Tell him you think the French goalkeeper isn't playing well.

f   Act embarassed! Say: Excuse me!

*RP 25a

You are at a disco in Dijon. Standing near you is someone of the opposite sex! Be brave. Start a conversation. It'll improve your French!

a   Greet the person and ask how they are.

b   Yes, you're English. Give the town you live in and the country.

c   You're on holiday, staying on a campsite. Ask if he/she lives in Dijon.

d   You've been studying French for five years.

e   You like modern music.

f   Ask if he/she wants to dance.

23a

j'habite à . . .
je m'appelle . . .

vous parlez . . . ?

je vais . . .
j'ai . . .
je suis . . .

à Lyon
en Angleterre/Ecosse
anglais(e)/écossais(e)
l'anglais

*24a

(You can often use *mais* at
the beginning of a French
phrase when "though" is at
the end of an English phrase.)

Oh, excusez-moi!

Il n'y a pas eu . . .
c'est un bon . . .

je crois que . . .

à mon avis

c'était une . . .
intéressante

beaucoup de fautes
match
première mi-temps
le gardien de but
l'équipe

les Français sont plus . . .
. . . essayé d'égaliser
. . . ne joue pas bien

peut-être parce que . . .

*25a

Voulez-vous danser?
Vous habitez . . . ?

bonsoir

j'aime la musique . . .
j'étudie le français depuis . . .

j'habite à . . . dans . . .
oui, je suis . . .
je suis dans un camping

TOPIC 6 Talking to friends

RP 26a	You've just arrived at your French friend's house. He/she shows you your room. Don't forget the present in your suitcase! (Your friend speaks first.)

a Tell your host that it's very nice. Thank him/her.

b You'd like a towel and some toothpaste.

c No, that's all.

d Say: Wait! Here's a present for you.

e Say: Go on! Open it!

RP 27a	It's the end of your first day with your French family. You've been talking French all evening. You're exhausted! But you have to be polite. (Your partner speaks first.)

a Say: yes, a little.

b You get up at 8.30.

c Normally, you have tea and toast.

d Announce that you're going to bed. Say: see you tomorrow.

e Refuse politely the offer of a drink. Say: see you tomorrow.

*RP 28a	You've just arrived at your French friend's house after a terrible car journey.

a Yes, you're late. Excuse yourself. You had a broken windscreen.

b You phoned the garage. You had to wait an hour and a half for the mechanic.

c It was on the motorway 20kms south of Paris. You were going at about 100kms an hour.

d Yes, you braked but it was raining. You skidded a little. You were lucky!

e Yes, you're tired and hungry.

f Say: thank-you.

26a

vas-y!
. . . ouvre-le!

attends!   je voudrais . . . s'il te plaît

une serviette
du dentifrice

non, c'est tout, merci   voici un cadeau pour toi

. . . super!

27a

je me lève à . . .
je prends . . .

oui, un peu   bon, je vais me coucher

bonne nuit
à demain!

non, merci!   du thé
un pain grillé

*28a

j'ai eu de la chance!

un pare-brise cassé

j'ai freiné   je suis en retard
j'ai eu un . . .
j'ai téléphoné au . . .   j'ai faim
j'ai dû attendre pendant . . .
j'ai dérapé   il pleuvait
je roulais à . . .
. . . kilomètres à l'heure   c'était à . . .
. . . au sud de Paris   c'était sur . . .
pour le mécanicien

TOPIC 6 Talking to friends

*RP 29a

It's the last day of your stay in France and you've been out shopping. You've bought two pairs of trousers, some perfume, a model of the Tour Eiffel and a huge garlic sausage! Show these to your French friend.

a Show him/her the trousers. They're for your brother. You hope he's going to like them.

b You bought them in a department store. Then show him/her the perfume. It's for your mother.

c You paid 65F.

d The Tour Eiffel is for your little sister. It's horrible but she'll like it.

e The sausage is for your father. You hate it!

f Nothing. You've no more money left!

*RP 30a

It's your last evening at your French friend's house. You decide not to go out. Your friend speaks first.

a Suggest watching television.

b You're not interested in that.

c No. It's too difficult.

d You only really like tennis.

e Ask if there are any films.

f You've already seen it.

g It's 8.30 now! Quick! Turn it on!

*29a

je n'ai plus d'argent!
j'ai payé . . .
des pantalons
du saucisson

rien

voici/voilà
une petite Tour Eiffel
du parfum

pour ma mère
pour mon frère
pour mon père
pour ma petite soeur

c'est affreux!

je déteste ça!
j'espère qu'il . . .

aimera ça

. . . dans un grand magasin

*30a

si on regardait la télé?
est-ce qu'il y a un film?

vite allume!
il est . . . maintenant!

c'est trop . . .
ça ne m'intéresse pas

vraiment, je n'aime que . . .
je l'ai déjà vu

RP 1b

Play the part of Madame Didot. You are expecting a phone call from an English boy/girl who is coming to stay with you for the summer. The phone rings. Does he/she say your number correctly? It should be 12–48–38–85.

a   Say yes. Ask who it is.

b   Recognise him/her. Enquire how he/she is.

c   You are well.

d   That's fine. You'll come and fetch him/her at the station.

e   Say goodbye.

RP 2b

Pretend that you are a French person who is very worried that your travelling companion may have left something behind on the boat. You are now waiting for the train. You speak first.

a   Ask him/her if she has the tickets.

b   Ask where his/her camera is.

c   And his/her suitcase! You can't see it!

d   Say: oh my goodness! You've left it on the boat!

★RP 3b

Play the part of the employee at the information desk in Orléans. You speak first.

a   Greet the customer.

b   Say the man has a problem. The next train is tomorrow morning. Leaves Orléans at 5.55.

c   No, it's direct.

d   Platform 3.

e   It arrives in La Rochelle at 7.08.

f   There is a hotel in the square. It isn't expensive.

1b

use *aller* when asking
how someone is (*ça va?*)

Qui est-ce?

c'est parfait!

*on viendra te chercher
à la gare*

2b

choose by thinking of
the word that comes after
them (e.g. *ta valise*)

je ne vois pas . . .
je l'ai laissé . . .

appareil-photo
oh, mon Dieu!

★3b

il a un problème, alors!

départ d'Orléans à . . .

. . . sur la place . . .

ce n'est pas cher

★RP 4b   Pretend you are serving behind the counter in the buffet de gare.

a   Tell him/her the phone box is over there, on the left, in the corner.

b   Act surprised. Tell him/her that there are no code numbers any more. You simply dial the number.

Now pretend that you are answering the phone. Your number is 51–34–45–67.

c   Yes (if your partner has got it right!).

d   Recognise the speaker and then ask if the train was a bit late.

e   The speaker hasn't understood. Repeat the question.

f   Say: OK, no problem. See you soon.

★RP 5b   Pretend you are a *contrôleur* on a train to Calais.

a   Ask the person for their ticket.

b   Say: yes.

c   Say: yes, of course!

d   Say: of course. Ask if he/she bought one.

e   Ask where he/she bought it.

f   Ask how much they paid?

g   Ask if it was a return ticket.

h   You're sorry but they are going to have to buy another ticket.

★RP 6b   Pretend that you are a French boy/girl meeting your partner at the station. Naturally you want to know what sort of journey he/she had.

a   Ask if he/she had a good journey.

b   Ask what time he/she left.

c   Ask if he/she caught the boat at Dover.

d   Ask if he/she had to change in Lille.

e   Did your partner have lunch?

f   What did your partner do to pass the time?

*4b

la cabine

dans le coin   il faut simplement composer
il n'y a plus d'indicatif   le . . .
le train était un peu en retard?   pas de problème
                                                                      à tout à l'heure

*5b

votre billet, s'il vous plaît
bien sûr!

en effet
effectivement

Est-ce que vous en avez   c'était un allet et . . .
acheté un?

combien avez-vous . . . ?

                              il faut acheter . . .

je regrette   où l'avez-vous acheté?

*6b

(You are asking your partner
about things they have already
done: you need **two words** for
the verb!)

tu as fait un . . . ?   Qu'est-ce que tu as fait
                                      pour . . . ?

                              à quelle heure tu es parti(e)?
tu as pris le . . . ?
tu as . . . ?   tu as dû changer . . . ?

| RP 7b | At the *station-service* a car has pulled up packed with people and luggage. Play the part of the attendant. The young person asking for petrol has a slight foreign accent so be sympathetic! |

a Say: yes sir, then tell him/her that it comes to 120F.

b Say: yes, certainly. Then tell him/her that the tyres and oil are OK.

c You're sorry but you don't have any maps.

d Say: Thank you, goodbye and have a good trip.

| RP 8b | Pretend you are the assistant in a camping shop. Your partner will ask you for things on his/her list. You should reply as follows: |

yes, you have blue sleeping bags

you have no folding chairs

your cheapest tent is 350F

bottle gas 14F

torch 22F

rucksack 140F

tea towels 10F each

it all comes to 276F, doesn't it?

| RP 9b | Pretend you are working in a grocer's shop. Your partner has a number of things he/she wants to buy. |

a Greet the customer.

b Say: here you are. Ask if there is anything else?

c Anything else?

d Does he/she want ground coffee?

e Anything else?

f Is that all?

g It comes to 162F 50.

h Say thank you and goodbye.

7b

l'huile

les pneus   *ça va*

je regrette . . .   *ça fait*

bon voyage!   *nous n'avons pas de . . .*

8b

nous avons/j'ai . . .

         sac à dos à . . . Francs

nous n'avons pas de . . .   *sacs de couchage en bleu*

      la moins chère coûte . . .

torchons   *cette torche-là à . . .*

bouteille de gaz

9b

        voilà, et avec ça?

      *vous le voulez comment le
café, moulu?*

ça fait   *c'est tout?*

★RP 10b

Your partner is helping you load the family car for the camping holiday. You are suggesting to one another where various things should go.

a The three cases, the rucksack, the air beds and the water carrier.

b Agree, then ask if there is room.

c Tell him/her there's a small box in the boot.

d Under the front seat.

e Say: yes. Oh no! the torch. Tell him/her you'll put it in the rucksack.

★RP 11b

You are trying to get your partner to help with the preparations for a camping holiday. Suggest any of the following (in any order!) and see what his/her reaction is. It might be an idea to write down what he/she agrees to!

a do the shopping

b check the camping equipment

c tidy the house

d look after the animals

e see to the car

f get the suitcases

g do the housework

h do the washing

i do the ironing

*10b

dans le coffre

les matelas de camping

il y a de la place . . . ?
. . . siège à l'avant

le bidon
la torche
une . . . boîte

sac à dos
les . . . valises
je vais la mettre . . .

*11b

vérifier les équipements
de camping
faire les courses
ranger la maison
chercher les valises
t'occuper des animaux

tu veux?
faire la lessive
t'occuper de la voiture
repasser le linge
faire le ménage

RP 12b

Play the part of the male warden on the campsite.

a Ask whether it is for a caravan or a tent.

b Ask how many nights it is for and how many people.

c Yes, there is room. Ask for their passports. Ask them to fill in this form. Say thank you.

d Thank the person.

RP 13b

Play the part of the female warden on the campsite.

a Greet the person.

b Ask how long it is for.

c You'll see. Yes, they are in luck. There is a place under the trees.

d Agree with him/her. Say: it's very hot!

*RP 14b

Pretend that you are working on a campsite in Avallon (Bourgogne). The phone rings. Your number is 84–37–82–08.

a If your partner has got the number right, say: yes.

b Yes, that's correct.

c Ask if it is for a caravan or a tent.

d Ask how she is travelling.

e And how many nights?

f That's fine, no problem. Check though: one tent, two adults, one night, no car. Is that right?

g Ask how that is written.

h Say: thank you Miss Townsend. You'll expect her on 26th July.

12b

c'est pour . . . ?   oui, il y a de la place

combien de nuits?

vos passeports . . .   Voulez-vous remplir cette fiche?

une caravane

une tente

13b

j'ai un emplacement

vous avez de la chance

sous les arbres

ah oui, il fait . . . !

c'est pour combien de   je vais regarder
temps?

*14b

c'est pour une . . . ?

oui, c'est ça   combien de nuits?
c'est ça?

et vous voyagez comment?   pas de problème
ça s'écrit comment?   pas de . . .

je vous attends le . . .

★RP 15b

  a Ask the person when he/she wrote.

  b Ask the person to wait a moment, you'll look at the list. Say: Ah yes, one night, one person, one tent.

  c Tell the person he/she has to pay now and leave the campsite before noon.

  d Add it up: one person, one night is 12F 50. Plus 5F for the tent. That comes to 17F 50.

  e Yes, but he/she must hurry. The restaurant closes at 9pm and it is now 8.20pm (use 24hr clock).

  f Say: Have a good meal!

★RP 16b

Pretend you are working on a French campsite. Someone has just pulled up in a car. They look tired so be sympathetic!

  a You're sorry but the campsite is full.

  b Say: Let's see . . . there's the Camping du Lac 10kms away.

  c Yes, it is a de-luxe campsite.

  d Of course. The number is 61–48–27–56.

  e Say: certainly. Then tell him/her to follow you.

  f Say: don't mention it.

★RP 17b

You are carrying out a survey on camping in France. Ask the following questions and write down the answers:

  a the person's name (ask them to spell the surname);

  b where they are from;

  c if it's their first time in France;

  d how many weeks holiday they have;

  e how long they are staying on this particular campsite;

  f if they are travelling alone;

  g do they have a tent or a caravan?

Don't forget to thank your interviewee! Oh, and his/her Cassoulet is beginning to burn!

*15b

vous avez écrit quand?

un moment . . .
je vais regarder la . . .
. . . une nuit . . . une tente

ça fait . . .
. . . avant midi
. . . maintenant
pour l'emplacement

le restaurant ferme à . . .

il faut payer . . .
il faut quitter le . . .
il faut se dépêcher

bon appétit!

---

*16b

je regrette
voyons

bien sûr!
certainement!

le camping est complet
c'est un camping de luxe
. . . à 10 kilomètres d'ici

il n'y a pas de quoi

voulez-vous bien me suivre?

---

*17b

Excusez-moi monsieur/mademoiselle

comment vous . . . ?
comment ça s'écrit s'il vous
plaît?

vous venez d'où?
vous voyagez seul(e)?

combien de temps allez vous
rester . . . ?
combien de semaines de
vacances . . . ?

Vous avez une caravane
ou . . . ?

c'est votre première
fois . . . ?

attention! votre Cassoulet
commence à brûler!

TOPIC 4 Leisure activities

RP 18b | Play the part of a receptionist in a French tourist office.

    a   Greet the tourist and ask if you can help.

    b   Say: here you are Monsieur/Mlle. It costs 9F.

    c   Give him/her the leaflet. It's free.

    d   Tell him/her it opens at 9am and closes at 5.30pm.

    e   Say: you're welcome, goodbye.

RP 19b | Play the part of the receptionist in a tourist office.

    a   Greet the customer and ask if you can help.

    b   There is a disco, it's open Tuesdays and Saturdays.

    c   Tell him/her it's in the rue d'Auxerre.

    d   It's open every night except Monday.

    e   Say: You're welcome.

★RP 20b | Pretend you are a French person just arrived at a campsite. You talk to one of the campers. Obviously you want to know something about the place. Write down what you are told. (You speak first). You want to know:

    a   how long he/she has been at the campsite;

    b   if it's a good campsite;

    c   what one can do there;

    d   if there is anything to do near the campsite?

Thank the person.

18b

> *je peux vous aider?*
> *je vous en prie*
>
> *le dépliant*
> *une carte de la région* *voilà!*
>
> *il ouvre à . . . et il ferme à . . .* *c'est gratuit*

19b

> *puis-je vous aider?*
>
> *c'est dans la . . .* *. . . sauf le lundi*
> *c'est ouvert le . . .*
>
> *il n'y a pas de quoi . . .*

★20b

> *excusez-moi . . .*
>
> *vous êtes dans ce camping*
> *depuis longtemps?*
> *c'est agréable comme* *qu'est-ce qu'on peut faire*
> *camping?* *ici?*
>
> *. . . dans les alentours?*

★RP 21b

Play the part of the receptionist in a tourist information office.

a   Greet the customer.

b   There's a water skiing school. It's called 'Touleski'.

c   You can hire equipment there. It's closed on Thursdays.

d   Oh yes, you think it's called 'Aux Meubles de Morvan'. There is a furniture exhibition there this week. Say: be careful though, it closes in the afternoon between 1pm and 3pm (use 24 hour clock).

e   Tell him/her it's very interesting!

f   Yes, that's right.

g   It's open all day, every day, between 10am to 6pm.

h   Say: you're welcome, goodbye.

★RP 22b

You are the receptionist in a tourist information office in Bourgogne. A young person comes in. You recognise him/her. He/she came in three days ago.

a   Greet him/her. Well then, was the water skiing good?

b   Tell him/her that there's lots of sports. Does he/she like horse riding?

c   There are some stables at Precy, 5 kms away on the road to Saulieu.

d   That's a bit difficult. People play that at the weekend. Tell him/her there's a château at Santenay. Is he/she interested?

e   It's 22kms away but it's interesting. There are chains and instruments of torture!

f   Yes, there's one in the square next to the bank.

g   Say: thank you and have a good day.

*21b

je vous en prie

une école de ski nautique
une exposition de meubles

ça s'appelle . . .

oui, c'est ça

mais attention!
je crois que . . .

c'est fermé . . .
c'est ouvert toute la journée

tous les jours entre . . .
cette semaine
pendant l'après-midi

*22b

Il y a . . .
il y en a un . . .

un château
un manège

à . . . kms sur la route de

ça vous intéresse?
alors! le ski . . . c'était bien?
. . . monter à cheval?

On y joue . . . le weekend
ça, c'est un peu difficile
c'est très . . . !

bonne journée!

dans
à côté de . . .
des chaînes
des instruments de torture

| RP 23b | Play the part of a French person travelling on a train. You want to strike up a conversation with another person in the compartment but you think he/she might not be French. |

a Say: excuse me, then ask if he/she is foreign.

b Tell him/her that your name is Christian/Christine Mathiot. Ask where he/she is going.

c Ask where in England (Scotland etc.) he/she lives.

d Tell him/her you're seventeen, then ask his/her age.

e You're going to Lyon as well. You're going to visit your aunt.

f Say: very little. Say that he/she speaks good French!

| *RP 24b | Play the part of a Frenchman watching a friendly football match between some French and English youngsters. You start to talk to someone on the sideline. |

a Ask what he/she thinks of the match.

b You think the English are playing better.

c Say: anyway, it's a friendly match.

d You think the English team is going to win.

e Say: There you are! The English have scored another goal!

f He's your son!

g Reassure the person. Tell him/her it doesn't matter. Anyway, it's true!

| *RP 25b | Play the part of a French boy/girl. You're at your local disco in Dijon. Your friends haven't turned up yet. Someone starts to speak to you. He/she has a slight foreign accent. |

a Say: good evening, tell the person you're fine. Ask if he/she is English.

b Ask if he/she is on holiday.

c Yes, you live in Dijon. You're at the lycée. Ask how long he/she has studied French.

d Ask what music he/she likes.

e You like jazz as well (as modern music).

f Yes! you'd certainly like to! But let's not be formal from now on.

23b

excusez-moi
vous parlez bien français!

très peu

je m'appelle . . .
j'ai . . .
je vais visiter . . .
je vais à . . .

. . . ma tante

Vous êtes étranger(ère)?
Où allez-vous?
Où habitez-vous . . . ?
Quel âge . . . ?

★24b

de toute façon

voilà!
ça ne fait rien
c'est vrai!
. . . mon fils!
. . . un match amical

qu'en pensez-vous
du . . . ?

je crois que . . .

les Anglais jouent mieux
. . . va gagner
. . . ont marqué un autre but

but
l'équipe
match

★25b

mais, on se tutoie, non?

vous êtes . . . ?
vous étudiez le français
depuis combien de temps?
quelle . . . aimez-vous?

oui, je veux bien!

j'aime aussi le . . .
. . . au lycée

TOPIC 6 Talking to friends

RP 26b

Pretend you are a French person whose English friend has just arrived. You speak first.

a Show your visitor his/her bedroom. Ask if it's OK.

b Ask if he/she needs anything?

c Nothing else? Some soap? Some shampoo?

d There's toothpaste in the bathroom. You'll go and get a towel.

e Show your appreciation!

f Say: Ah, a poster of Charles and Diana! Thank your friend.

RP 27b

Play the part of a French person whose English friend has just arrived today. It's evening. (You speak first.)

a Enquire if he/she is tired.

b Ask at what time he/she normally gets up.

c Ask what he/she has for breakfast.

d Repeat what he/she has told you about breakfast and say that's fine.

e Say good night. Ask if he/she wants to drink something.

★RP 28b

Play the part of a French person. You've been waiting for your English friend to arrive. They're late and you're worried because he/she is coming by car.

a Say: There you are at last!

b Show concern! Ask what he/she did.

c Where did it happen?

d Show even more concern! What did he/she do? Brake?

e Say: anyway you're here now. Then ask if he/she is tired.

f The dinner's ready. You can eat straight away.

26b

> est-ce que tu as besoin de quelque
> chose?
>
> rien d'autre?
>
> voici ta chambre
>
> il y a . . . dans la . . .   ah, une affiche de . . .
> je vais chercher une . . .
>
> ça va?
>
> du savon?
> du shampooing?
> du dentifrice   c'est très gentil!
> une serviette

27b

> qu'est-ce que tu prends . . . ?
>
> tu es fatigué(e)?   . . . pour le petit déjeuner?
> tu veux boire quelque   . . . tu te lèves d'habitude?
> chose?
> à quelle heure . . . ?
>
> bonne nuit!
>
> oui, oui, très bien!

*28b

> Te voilà enfin!
>
> qu'est-ce que tu as fait?   tout de suite
> Tu as freiné?   oh mon dieu!
> Où est-ce que ça s'est passé?   de toute façon
>
> tu es là maintenant
> tu es fatigué . . . ?
>
> on peut manger . . .   le dîner est prêt

*RP 29b

Pretend you are a French person who has had an English friend staying with you. He/She has just come staggering in from some last minute shopping.

a   Say: oh yes, orange, they're very nice! Ask where he/she bought them.

b   Say: that's nice. How much was it?

c   That's not too dear.

d   It's not horrible. You like it.

e   Tell him/her it smells good! And what about for himself/herself?

f   Feel sorry for him/her. Say: you poor thing!

*RP 30b

Play the part of a French person. Your English friend is leaving tomorrow morning, early. You've decided to stay in. But just sitting around might get boring! You speak first.

a   Ask what you're going to do tonight.

b   You agree. There's the local news now on Antenne 2.

c   There's a quiz programme on TF1.

d   Well, after the news there's some sport. It's golf.

e   Get a little annoyed. Say: you're difficult!

f   At 9pm (24 hour clock) there's Towering Inferno on Antenne 2.

g   On TF1 at 8.30 there's Dallas.

*29b

orange
ce n'est pas cher
. . . affreux
j'aime ça
ça sent bon!
ils sont beaux!
c'est beau/joli

c'était combien?
où as-tu acheté ça?
et pour toi-même?

oh le/la pauvre!

*30b

que tu es difficile!

d'accord
eh bien . . .

sur TF1

après . . .

La Tour Infernale
Dallas
Les Actualités Régionales
Des Chiffres et des Lettres

il y a . . .

Qu'est-ce qu'on fait ce soir?

TAPESCRIPT

TOPIC 1 Travel

<table>
<tr><td>RP1</td><td>You are phoning a French family to give them the details of your arrival.</td></tr>
</table>

a Say hello and ask if it's number 12–48–38–85. * * *
Allô c'est le 12–48–38–85?
Oui, c'est ça, qui est-ce?

b Tell her who you are. * * *
C'est Louise Townsend.
Ah bonjour Louise, ça va?

c You are well. Enquire how she is. * * *
Oui ça va bien merci, et vous?
Ça va bien merci.

d You're arriving on the 15th June, 3pm at the Gare du Nord. * * *
J'arrive le quinze juin à 15 heures à la gare du Nord.
C'est parfait, Louise, on viendra te chercher à la gare.

e Thank her. Tell her you'll see her soon. Say: goodbye. * * *
Merci. A bientôt. Au revoir madame.
Au revoir.

RP2 You are travelling with a French friend who is very worried that you may have left something behind. You are standing on the platform waiting for the train.

a Tu as les billets?
Tell her they're in your bag. ***
Les voilà! dans mon sac.

b Et où est ton appareil-photo?
It's there, on the seat! ***
Le voilà, sur le siège!

c Et ta valise! je ne vois pas ta valise!
Tell her, it's over there, by the wall! ***
La voilà! contre le mur!
Ah oui.
Tell her she's very edgy today. ***
Que tu es nerveuse aujourd'hui!

d Ask where her passport is. ***
Où est ton passeport?
Oh mon Dieu! je l'ai laissé sur le bateau!

*RP3	At Orléans station you meet an Englishman who needs your help. He can't speak French. He's going to La Rochelle. He's missed his connection.

Go to the information desk

a Bonjour mademoiselle.
Tell the employee what's happened. ***
Ce monsieur ne parle pas français. Il va à La Rochelle et il a raté sa correspondance.
Oh là là.
Ask the time of the next train. ***
Le prochain train, c'est à quelle heure?
Il a un problème alors! Le prochain train, c'est demain matin.
Départ d'Orléans à 5 heures 55.

b Show concern. ***
Oh, mon Dieu!
Ask if he will have to change. ***
Il doit changer?
Non, c'est direct.

c Ask which platform. ***
Quel quai s'il vous plaît?
Quai numéro trois, mademoiselle.

d Ask what time it arrives in La Rochelle. ***
A quelle heure est-ce qu'il arrive à La Rochelle?
A sept heures huit.

e Ask if there is a hotel nearby. Not too expensive. ***
Est-ce qu'il y a un hôtel près d'ici. Pas trop cher?
Oui, il y a un hôtel sur la place. Ce n'est pas cher.

f Thank the assistant. ***
Merci, monsieur.
Je vous en prie, mademoiselle.

*RP4

You've missed your connection to Marseille. You need to phone the people you'll be staying with so you go to the *buffet de gare*.

a Ask if you can make a phone call. ***
On peut téléphoner d'ici?
Oui, la cabine est là, à gauche, dans le coin.

b Thank him then ask for the code for Marseille. ***
Merci monsieur. Quel est l'indicatif pour Marseille?
L'indicatif? mais il n'y a plus d'indicatif. Il faut simplement composer le numéro.

c Oh yes, you'd forgotten. ***
Ah oui, j'avais oublié!

d Ask if that's 51–34–45–67. ***
Allô, c'est le 51–34–45–67?
Oui, c'est ça. Qui est-ce?

e Say who you are and that you're still in Lyon. ***
C'est Louise Townsend. Je suis encore à Lyon.
Ah oui, Louise, c'est toi. A Lyon? le train était un peu en retard alors.

f Ask her to repeat. You haven't understood. ***
Répétez s'il vous plaît Madame. Je n'ai pas compris.
Oui, le train était en retard?

g Yes, exactly. You missed your connection. You'll arrive at 18.35. ***
Oui c'est ça. J'ai raté la correspondance. J'arrive à 18.35.
Très bien, Louise, pas de problème. A tout à l'heure.

h Say: yes goodbye, see you later. ***
Oui, au revoir, à tout à l'heure.

*RP5 — You are on a train travelling from Lille to Calais. The *contrôleur* comes up to you. You search for your ticket and you start getting that sinking feeling!

a Votre billet monsieur.
Tell him you think it's in your bag. There it is! ***
Il est dans mon sac, je crois. Le voilà!
No. that's a luggage ticket.
Ah non, c'est un ticket de consigne.

b Oui monsieur.
You try again. You've got it! No, it's a metro ticket! ***
Le voilà. Ah non, c'est un ticket de métro.

c Oui, monsieur, effectivement.
Admit to him you can't find your ticket. ***
Je ne trouve pas mon billet monsieur.

d En effet monsieur. Est-ce que vous en avez acheté un?
Act offended! Say: of course! You've lost it that's all! ***
Mais, bien sûr, je l'ai perdu voilà tout!

e Bien sûr. Et où est-ce que vous avez acheté ce billet?
Tell him you bought it in Lille. ***
Je l'ai acheté à Lille.

f Et combien vous avez payé?
28 Francs. You think. ***
28F, je crois.

g 28 Francs. Et c'était un aller et retour?
No, a single. ***
Non, un aller simple.

h Je regrette monsieur mais il vous faut acheter un autre billet.
Plead with him! Tell him: that's impossible! Ask him to be reasonable. ***
Mais ça, ce n'est pas possible! Essayez de comprendre, monsieur!

*RP6 You have finally arrived at your French destination and you are met by your host family. Your friend wants to know what sort of a journey you had.

a Eh bien, tu as fait un bon voyage?
Tell her it wasn't bad. A bit tiring. ***
Oh pas mal, un peu fatigant.

b A quelle heure tu es parti?
This morning you left at about 8. ***
Ce matin je suis partie vers 8 heures.

c Et tu as pris le bateau à Douvres?
Yes, the sea was fairly calm. ***
Oui, la mer était assez calme.

d Est-ce que tu as dû changer à Lille?
That's right, and you had to wait 40 minutes for the connection. ***
Oui, et j'ai dû attendre 40 minutes pour la correspondance.

e Tu as déjeuné, j'espère!
You bought a sandwich from the station buffet. ***
J'ai acheté un sandwich au buffet de la gare.

f Et qu'est-ce que tu as fait pour passer le temps?
You talked to a French boy. You read a magazine. ***
J'ai bavardé avec un jeune français. J'ai lu un magazine.

TOPIC 2 Preparations for a holiday

RP7

You are finally off on holiday with your French family. However you must first stop to fill up with petrol. Your hosts insist that you ask for it.

a Ask the attendant for 25 litres of four star petrol. ***
25 litres de super s'il vous plaît.
Oui, mademoiselle, ça fait 120F.

b Ask him to check the tyres and the oil. ***
Voulez-vous vérifier les pneus et l'huile s'il vous plaît?
Oui mademoiselle, tout de suite. Bon . . . les pneus et l'huile ça va.

c Ask if you can buy a map at the garage. ***
Est-ce qu'on peut acheter une carte ici?
Non, je regrette, nous n'avons pas de cartes.

d Say thank you and goodbye. ***
Merci monsieur, au revoir.
Au revoir et bon voyage!

RP8	You have decided to go to the camping shop to buy equipment. You have the list of the things you need.

a Greet the shopkeeper then ask if he has sleeping bags in blue or green. ***
Bonjour monsieur, avez-vous des sacs de couchage en bleu ou en vert?
Oui nous avons des sacs de couchage en bleu.

b Say thank you, and you want two tea towels. ***
Merci et deux torchons s'il vous plaît.
Voilà des torchons à dix francs.

c Now you want a cheap tent. ***
Et une tente, pas trop chère.
Nous avons de petites tentes, des canadiennes, à 350F.
No, it's too expensive. Does he have anything cheaper? ***
Non, c'est trop cher, avez-vous quelque chose de moins cher?
Non mademoiselle, je regrette.

d *Ask for the bottle gas next.* ***
Et une bouteille de gaz.
Voilà, une bouteille de gaz.

e *Now ask for a small rucksack (not more than 180 Francs).* ***
Et un petit sac à dos, s'il vous plaît.
Alors, le plus petit, et le moins cher coûte 140F. Ça va?

f Yes, that's fine. Oh yes and a torch. ***
C'est parfait. Ah oui, et une torche.
Une torche. Oui nous avons celle-là à 22 Francs.

g Say: yes, thank you. Then ask how much it all comes to. ***
Oui, merci. Ça fait combien?
Alors, voyons, ça fait . . . euh 276 Francs, mademoiselle.

RP9

You go shopping for the food. You can't drive to the supermarket so you go down to the local épicerie.

a Greet the young girl in the shop. ***
Bonjour Mademoiselle.
Bonjour monsieur.

b Ask for eight bottles of mineral water and four bottles of red wine. ***
Je voudrais huit bouteilles d'eau minérale et quatre bouteilles de vin rouge, s'il vous plaît.
Voilà monsieur. Et avec ça?

c Ask for some cheese: a creamy one and a blue cheese. ***
Et du fromage s'il vous plaît. Un Camembert et un Bleu de Bresse.
Voilà. Et avec ça?

d You want 400gms of pâté and some coffee. ***
400gms de pâté et du café.
Vous le voulez comment le café, moulu?

e You want ground coffee. ***
Oui, oui, moulu.
Voilà. Et avec ça?

f You also want some drinking chocolate. ***
Je voudrais aussi du chocolat en poudre.
C'est tout?

g Yes. Ask how much it comes to. ***
Oui, ça fait combien?
Ça fait 162F 50, s'il vous plaît, monsieur.

h Say thank you and goodbye. ***
Merci mademoiselle. Au revoir.
Au revoir monsieur. Merci.

| ***RP10** | You are helping your French friend load the family car for the camping holiday. |

a Ask what you should put in the boot. ***
Qu'est-ce qu'on met dans le coffre?
Dans le coffre. Euh voyons . . . les trois valises, le sac à dos, les matelas de camping et le bidon d'eau.

b There isn't enough room for the water carrier. Suggest putting it under the back seat. ***
Il n'y a pas assez de place pour le bidon. Si on le mettait sous le siège arrière?
Bon, d'accord. Il y a de la place?

c Yes, that's fine. Ask where you should put the tin opener. ***
Oui, ça va. Où est-ce qu'on met l'ouvre-boîtes?
Euh . . . donc il y a une petite boîte dans le coffre pour des trucs comme ça.

d OK. Ask where the rope should go? ***
Bon. Et la corde?
La corde? Tu peux la mettre sous le siège à l'avant.

e Ask if that's all. ***
C'est tout?
Oui, c'est tout. ah non, la torche, je vais la mettre dans le sac à dos.

| ***RP11** | You are about to go on a camping holiday with your French family. Your friend is trying to get you to help with the preparations. |

a   Tu veux m'aider un peu? Tu veux faire les courses?
Yes, you'll gladly do that. * * *
Oui, je veux bien.

b   Et tu veux faire la lessive?
You don't like doing that very much. * * *
Oh, je n'aime pas faire ça, vraiment.

c   Bon, d'accord. Alors est-ce que tu veux ranger la maison?
Mmm. Say you'd prefer to look after the animals. * * *
Oui, mais je préfère m'occuper des animaux.

d   D'accord. Qu'est-ce qu'il y a encore?
Offer to check the camping equipment. * * *
Est-ce que je peux vérifier les équipements de camping?
Bien sûr! Vas-y. Ils sont dans la cave.

| RP12 | You have arrived at a campsite. |

a Greet the warden and ask if he has any room. ***
Bonjour monsieur. Avez-vous de la place s'il vous plaît?
C'est pour une caravane ou pour une tente?

b It's for one tent. ***
C'est pour une tente.
Pour combien de nuits et pour combien de personnes?

c For one night and for two people. ***
Pour une nuit et pour deux personnes.
Bon, alors oui, il y a de la place. Est-ce que vous avez vos passeports? Voilà. Et voulez vous remplir cette fiche?

d Say: yes certainly, then thank him. ***
Oui, bien sûr. Merci mademoiselle.
Merci mademoiselle.

TOPIC 3 Campsite

RP13 You have arrived at a campsite. You spot a young lady who you think might be the warden.

a Greet her. ***
Bonjour mademoiselle.
Bonjour monsieur.

b Ask if she has any room. It's for a family of six with two tents. ***
Avez-vous de la place? C'est pour une famille de six avec deux tentes.
C'est pour combien de temps?

c It's for four days. Until August 14th. ***
C'est pour quatre jours. Jusqu'au 14 août.
Je vais regarder . . . attendez . . . oui vous avez de la chance.
J'ai un emplacement sous les arbres.

d Thank her then say: it's hot today. ***
Merci mademoiselle. Il fait chaud aujourd'hui!
Ah oui, il fait chaud!

*RP14

Your name is Louise Townsend and you are on a cycling holiday with a friend. You don't want to arrive at the next campsite only to find it full. Make a phone call.

a Ask if that's 84–37–82–08. *******
Allô c'est le 84–37–82–08?
Oui, c'est ça.

b Ask if it's the Mogador campsite. *******
C'est le camping Mogador?
Oui.

c You'd like to book a place for the day after tomorrow. The 26th July. *******
Je voudrais réserver un emplacement pour après-demain, le 26 juillet.
C'est pour une caravane ou pour une tente?

d It's for a small tent. *******
C'est pour une petite tente.
Et vous voyagez comment, en voiture?

e No, on bikes. You're two adults. *******
Non, à vélo. Nous sommes deux adultes.
Bon, euh . . . c'est pour combien de nuits mademoiselle?

f One night only. *******
Une nuit seulement.
Très bien, pas de problème. Donc: une tente, deux adultes, une nuit, pas de voiture. C'est ça?

g Say: Yes, then give him your name. *******
Oui monsieur. Je m'appelle Louise Townsend.
Ah! Ça s'écrit comment?

h Spell Townsend. Tell him that's your surname. *******
T-o-w-n-s-e-n-d. Ça c'est mon nom de famille.
Merci Mademoiselle Townsend. Je vous attends le 26 juillet.

i Say: thank you and goodbye.
Merci monsieur, au revoir.

---

*RP15 You have arrived at a campsite. You know there shouldn't be any problem because you phoned yesterday. But you never know!

a Greet the warden and tell her you made a booking in the name of Thompson. ***
Bonjour madame. J'ai fait une réservation au nom de Thompson.
Vous avez écrit quand?

b *No, you phoned yesterday.* ***
Non, j'ai téléphoné hier.
Un moment s'il vous plaît monsieur. Je vais regarder la liste. Ah oui, une nuit, une personne, une tente. Monsieur Thompson.

c Yes, that's right. ***
Oui, c'est ça.
Alors il faut payer maintenant et il faut quitter le camping avant midi.

d Say: yes, of course. Ask what the price is. ***
Oui, oui, bien sûr! Ça fait combien?
Donc . . . euh . . . une personne, une nuit c'est 12F 50. Plus 5F pour l'emplacement. Ça fait 17F 50.

e Ask if there is a restaurant. ***
Est-ce qu'il y a un restaurant?
You're very tired and you don't want to cook this evening. ***
Je suis très fatigué et je n'ai pas envie de cuisiner ce soir.
Oui, mais il faut se dépêcher. Le restaurant ferme à 21 heures et il est maintenant . . . euh . . . . 20 heures 20.

f Thank her and say: good evening. ***
Merci madame, bonsoir.
Bonsoir monsieur et bon appétit.

TOPIC 3 Campsite

*RP16   You've arrived at a campsite after a hard day's drive. You're looking forward to a shower and a meal.

   a   Greet the warden and ask if he has room for a caravan. ***
Bonjour monsieur. Avez-vous de la place pour une caravane?
Non madame, je regrette. Le camping est complet.

   b   Express annoyance. Ask if there is another campsite nearby. ***
Oh zut! y a-t-il un autre camping près d'ici?
Euh . . . voyons . . . il y a le Camping du Lac à dix kilomètres d'ici.

   c   Ask if it's a comfortable campsite. You've done a lot of miles today. ***
C'est un camping tout confort? J'ai fait pas mal de kilomètres aujourd'hui!
Oui madame. C'est un camping deluxe.

   d   Ask if he can give you the phone number. ***
Pouvez-vous me donner le numéro de téléphone s'il vous plaît.
Certainement. Oui, voilà, c'est le 61–48–27–56.

   e   Ask if you can phone from the campsite. You'll pay of course. ***
Puis-je téléphoner d'ici? Je payerai bien sûr.
Oui, oui, certainement madame. Voulez-vous bien me suivre?

   f   Thank him. ***
Merci monsieur.
Il n'y a pas de quoi, madame.

*RP17

You are staying on a French campsite. Whilst heating up some tinned Cassoulet for your lunch you are approached by a young Frenchman who is carrying out a survey on camping in France. He's going to ask you some questions.

a Bonjour mademoiselle, excusez-moi, je fais un sondage sur le camping en France. Voulez-vous bien répondre à quelques questions. Oui? Merci. Alors . . . comment vous appelez-vous?
Your name is Jane Robertson. ***
Je m'appelle Jane Robertson.

b Comment ça s'écrit s'il vous plaît?
Spell the surname. ***
R-o-b-e-r-t-s-o-n.

c Bon . . . Robertson, Jane. Et vous venez d'où?
You're from Glasgow in Scotland. ***
Je suis de Glasgow. En Ecosse.

d C'est votre première fois en France?
Yes it's your first time. ***
Oui c'est ma première fois.

e Première fois . . . et combien de semaines de vacances avez-vous?
You have two weeks holiday. ***
J'ai deux semaines.

f Combien de temps allez-vous rester ici, dans ce camping?
You're staying for three days. ***
Je reste ici trois jours.

g Et vous voyagez seule?
You're with a group of friends. ***
Non, je suis avec un groupe d'amis.

h Ah bon . . . avec groupe . . . et vous avez une tente ou une caravane?
You have a small tent. ***
J'ai une petite tente.

i Très bien, mademoiselle Robertson. Je vous remercie. Oh! attention! votre Cassoulet commence à brûler!
What's he saying? React in French! ***
Ah? quoi? . . . oh zut!
Ecoutez, moi je connais pas mal la région. Qu'est-ce que vous faites ce soir? Moi je voudrais bien . . .

RP18 You are at the tourist office.

a Greet the man behind the desk. * * *
Bonjour monsieur.
Bonjour mademoiselle. Je peux vous aider?

b You want a map of the region. * * *
Avez-vous une carte de la région?
Oui, voilà une carte de la région. C'est 9F.

c You'd also like a leaflet about the town. * * *
Et je voudrais aussi un dépliant sur la ville.
Voilà mademoiselle. C'est gratuit.

d Ask what time the museum opens. * * *
A quelle heure ouvre le musée?
Donc, il ouvre à 9 heures et il ferme à 17 heures 30.

e Say: thank you and goodbye. * * *
Merci, monsieur, au revoir.
Je vous en prie. Au revoir.

RP19   You go to the tourist office. You've had enough of culture. Now, how about some fun!

a   Greet the woman behind the desk. ✱✱✱
Bonjour madame.
Bonjour monsieur. Puis-je vous aider?

b   Yes, ask if there is a disco in town. ✱✱✱
Oui, est-ce qu'il y a une discothèque en ville?
Une discothèque? Oui, c'est ouvert le mardi et le samedi.

c   Now ask where the cinema is. ✱✱✱
Et, où est le cinéma?
C'est dans la rue d'Auxerre.

d   Ask if it's open every evening. ✱✱✱
C'est ouvert tous les soirs?
Euh, tous les soirs sauf le lundi.

e   Thank her. ✱✱✱
Merci madame.
Il n'y a pas de quoi.

---

*RP20 You are at the entrance to the campsite where you have been staying for a few days. A French woman who has just arrived starts asking you some questions about the place.

a Excusez-moi, vous êtes dans ce camping depuis longtemps?
Tell her you've been there for three days. ***
Je suis là depuis trois jours.

b Et c'est agréable comme camping?
Yes, it's a good campsite. Pleasant. ***
Oui, oui. C'est très bien. C'est agréable.

c Qu'est-ce qu'on peut faire ici?
Tell her there's a swimming pool and a games room. ***
Eh bien il y a une piscine et une salle de jeux.

d Et dans les alentours?
There's a lake 500 metres away. ***
Il y a le lac à 500 mètres.
Ah!
You can fish, go sailing, canoeing. ***
On peut pêcher, faire de la voile, faire du canoë.

e Merci mademoiselle.
Say: You're welcome. ***
Je vous en prie, madame.

---

*RP21 You want to plan the next four days of your holiday. Today is Monday 13th June. Here's the tourist information office. In you go!

a Greet the young woman behind the desk. ***
Bonjour mademoiselle.
Bonjour monsieur.

b Tell her you're interested in water skiing. Can you do this at the lake? ***
Je suis un passionné du ski nautique. Est-ce qu'on peut en faire au lac?
Oui, il y a une école de ski nautique. Ça s'appelle Touleski.

c Ask if you can hire the equipement there. ***
Est-ce qu'on peut y louer l'équipement?
Oui, oui, vous pouvez le louer sur place. Mais c'est fermé le jeudi.

d Also, you've heard of an antiques shop in Brassy. ***
Oui, et puis j'ai entendu parler d'un magasin d'antiquités à Brassy.
Oui, je crois que ça s'appelle 'Aux meubles de Morvan'. Il y a une exposition de meubles cette semaine. Mais attention, c'est fermé l'après-midi entre 13 heures et 15 heures.

e Ask if it's interesting. ***
C'est intéressant?
Ah oui, c'est très intéressant.

f Check the date of the exhibition. The 13th – 18th June? ***
Donc, c'est du 13 juin jusqu'au 18?
Oui, c'est ça.

g Now ask for the opening hours of the swimming pool in Luzy. ***
Quelles sont les heures d'ouverture de la piscine à Luzy?
C'est ouvert toute la journée, tous les jours, entre 10 heures et 18 heures.

h Say: you've been very kind, thank you, goodbye. ***
Vous avez été très aimable, mademoiselle . . . merci. Au revoir!
Je vous en prie. Au revoir.

*RP22 It's your last few days in Bourgogne so you want to make the most of them. Perhaps some more sport. Oh yes, and there's the disco tomorrow and camping hasn't done much for your hairstyle. Go to the information office.

a Greet the young woman again. ***
Bonjour mademoiselle.
Ah bonjour monsieur! Et alors . . . le ski nautique, c'était bien?

b Tell her you enjoyed it. Difficult though! ***
Oui, je me suis beaucoup amusé! Mais c'est difficile hein?
Oui, un peu, oui, au début.
Ask what other sports you can do in the area. ***
Quels sont les autres sports qu'on peut faire ici?
Il y a beaucoup de sports. Vous aimez monter à cheval?

c Tell her you'd like that. You've done it in England. ***
Oui, j'aimerais bien faire ça. J'en ai fait en Angleterre.
Alors, il y a un manège à Precy. A 5 kilomètres sur la route de Saulieu.

d Say: thank you. Good idea. Then ask where you can play French bowls. ***
Merci, Bonne idée. Où est-ce qu'on peut jouer à la pétanque?
Ça, c'est un peu difficile. On y joue le weekend. Il y a un château à Santenay. Ça vous intéresse?

e Say: a little. Is it far? ***
Oui, un peu. C'est loin?
C'est à 22 kilomètres mais c'est très intéressant. Il y a des chaînes et des instruments de torture!

f You agree to go. Oh yes, ask if there's a cheap hairdresser's in town. ***
Bon, d'accord. Est-ce qu'il y a un coiffeur pas trop cher en ville?
Oui, il y en a sur la place à côté de la banque.

g Thank her and say goodbye. ***
Merci, mademoiselle. Au revoir.
Au revoir et bonne journée!

TOPIC 5 Talking to strangers

RP23 You're travelling through France by train. A French person sitting opposite you starts talking to you.

a Excusez-moi, vous êtes étranger?
Tell her you're English. Introduce yourself. * * *
Je suis anglais. Je m'appelle Ian Townsend.

b Je m'appelle Christine Mathiot. Où allez-vous?
You're going to Lyon. * * *
Je vais à Lyon.

c Et où habitez-vous en Angleterre . . . vous êtes d'où?
Tell her you live in Leamington Spa. In the Midlands. * * *
J'habite à Leamington Spa. Dans le centre de l'Angleterre.

d Moi, j'ai dix-sept ans. Et vous, quel âge avez-vous?
Tell her you're sixteen. * * *
J'ai seize ans.

e Je vais à Lyon aussi. Je vais visiter ma tante.
Ask if she speaks English.
Vous parlez anglais?

f Très peu. Mais vous, vous parlez bien français!
Say: thank you. * * *
Merci.

*RP24 You are on the sideline watching a football match between French and English youngsters. The second half has just started. A middle-aged Frenchman starts talking to you.

a Qu'en pensez-vous du match?
You think it's a good match. It was an interesting first half. ***
C'est un bon match à mon avis. C'était une première mi-temps intéressante.

b Moi, je crois que les Anglais jouent mieux.
Perhaps because the French are younger. ***
Peut-être parce que les Français sont plus jeunes.

c Oui, peut-être. De toute façon c'est un match amical.
You agree. There haven't been many fouls.
Oui, il n'y a pas eu beaucoup de fautes.

d Je crois que l'équipe anglaise va gagner.
The French team is trying to equalise though. ***
Oui, mais l'équipe française essaye d'égaliser.

e Voilà! les Anglais ont marqué un autre but!
Tell him you think the French goalkeeper isn't playing very well. ***
Je crois que le gardien de but français ne joue pas bien.

f Euh . . . c'est mon fils!
Act embarassed! Apologise. ***
Oh! excusez-moi monsieur!

g Oh, ça ne fait rien. De toute façon c'est vrai.

| ***RP25** | You are at a Disco in Dijon. Standing near you is someone of the opposite sex! Be brave. Start a conversation. It'll improve your French! |

a Greet him. Ask how he is. ***
Bonsoir. Ça va?
Bonsoir. Ça va, oui. Vous êtes anglaise?

b Yes, you're English. Tell him the town you live in and the county. ***
Oui, je suis anglaise. J'habite à Leamington, dans le Warwickshire.
Vous êtes en vacances?

c Yes. You're on holiday, staying on a campsite. ***
Oui, je suis en vacances. Je suis dans un camping.
Ah oui?
Ask if he lives in Dijon. ***
Vous habitez à Dijon?
Oui, ici à Dijon. Je suis au lycée. Euh, vous étudiez le français depuis combien de temps?

d You've been studying French for five years. ***
J'étudie le français depuis 5 ans.
Huh-huh. Et quelle musique aimez-vous?

e You like modern music. ***
J'aime la musique moderne.
Moi, j'aime le jazz aussi.

f Ask if he wants to dance! ***
Voulez-vous danser?
Oui, je veux bien. Mais, écoute, on se tutoie, non?

RP26	It's your last evening at your friend's house. You decide not to go out.

a Qu'est-ce qu'on fait ce soir?
Suggest watching television. ***
Euh . . . et si on regardait la télé?

b D'accord. Voyons . . . euh . . . il y a Les Actualités Régionales maintenant, sur Antenne 2.
You're not interested in that. ***
Ah non ça ne m'intéresse pas.

c Il y a Des Chiffres et Des Lettres sur TF1.
No. It's too difficult. ***
Non, c'est trop difficile.

d Eh bien, après les Actualités il y a du sport . . . du golf.
You only really like tennis. ***
Vraiment je n'aime que le tennis.

e Oh que tu es difficile!
Ask if there are any films. ***
Est-ce qu'il y a un film?

f Oui, à 21 heures sur Antenne 2 il y a La Tour Infernale . . . tu connais ça, la Tour Infernale?
You've already seen it. ***
Je l'ai déjà vu.

g Et sur TF1 à 20 heures 30 il y a Dallas.
It' 8.30 now! Quick! Turn it on! ***
Mais il est huit heures et demie maintenant! Vite! Allume!

| RP27 | It's the end of your first day with your French family. You've been talking French all evening. Now you're exhausted! But don't forget to be polite. |

a Tu es fatiguée?
Say: yes, a little. ***
Oui, un peu.

b A quelle heure tu te lèves d'habitude le matin?
You get up at 8.30. ***
Je me lève à huit heures et demie.

c Et qu'est-ce que tu prends pour le petit déjeuner?
Normally you have tea and toast. ***
D'habitude je prends du thé et du pain grillé.

d Du thé et du pain grillé? Oui, oui, très bien.
Announce that you're going to bed. Say: good night. ***
Bon, je vais me coucher. Bonne nuit.

e Bonne nuit, ma chère. Tu veux boire quelque chose?
Refuse politely. Then say: see you tomorrow. ***
Non, merci. Bonne nuit. A demain!

TOPIC 6 Talking to friends

*RP28 You've just arrived at your French friend's house after a terrible car journey.

a Ah! te voilà enfin!
Yes, you're late. Apologise. You had a broken windscreen. ***
Oui, excuse-moi! J'ai eu un pare-brise cassé.

b Oh mon Dieu! Qu'est-ce que tu as fait?
You phoned a garage. You had to wait an hour and a half for the mechanic. ***
J'ai téléphoné au garage. J'ai dû attendre pendant une heure et demie pour le mécanicien!

c Où est-ce que ça s'est passé?
It was on the motorway. 20kms south of Paris. ***
C'était sur l'autoroute, à vingt kilomètres au sud de Paris.
Ah!
You were going at about 100kms an hour. ***
Je roulais à 100 kilomètres à l'heure.

d Oh là là! à cent? Qu'est-ce que tu as fait? Tu as freiné?
Yes, you braked but it was raining. You skidded a little. ***
Oui, j'ai freiné, mais il pleuvait et j'ai dérapé un peu.
Ah oui, évidemment!
Yes, you were lucky!
Oui, j'ai eu de la chance!

e De toute façon tu es là maintenant. Tu es fatigué?
Yes, you're tired and hungry. ***
Oui, je suis fatigué et j'ai faim!

f Alors, le dîner est prêt. On peut manger tout de suite.
Say: Thank you. ***
Merci.

<table>
<tr><td>***RP29**</td><td>It's your last day in France and you've been out shopping. Show your French friend all the things you've bought.</td></tr>
</table>

a   Show her the trousers. They're for your brother. ***
Voici des pantalons pour mon frère.
Hum . . . en orange . . . ils sont beaux!
Yes, you hope he's going to like them. ***
Oui, j'espère qu'il aimera ça.
Où as-tu acheté ça?

b   You bought them in a department store. ***
Dans un grand magasin.
Show her the perfume. It's for your mother. ***
Et voici du parfum pour ma mère.
Ah c'est joli ça. C'était combien?

c   You paid 65F. ***
J'ai payé 65F.
Ce n'est pas cher.

d   The little Tour Eiffel is for your little sister. ***
Et voici une petite Tour Eiffel pour ma petite soeur.
Ah!
It's horrible but she'll like it. ***
C'est affreux mais elle aimera ça.
Non, ce n'est pas affreux! Moi j'aime bien ça!

e   The sausage is for your father. You hate it! ***
Le saucisson est pour mon père. Moi, je déteste ça!
Hum . . . ça sent bon! Et pour toi-même?

f   Nothing. You've no more money left! ***
Rien. Je n'ai plus d'argent!
Oh, la pauvre!

TOPIC 6 Talking to friends

You've arrived at your French friend's house. She shows you your room. Don't forget the present in the suitcase!

a Alors, Ian, voici ta chambre. Ça va?
  Tell her it's very nice. Thank her. *******
  Ah oui, elle est super!

b Est-ce que tu as besoin de quelque chose?
  You'd like a towel and some toothpaste. *******
  Je voudrais une serviette et du dentifrice s'il te plaît.

c Rien d'autre? Du savon . . . du shampooing?
  No, that's all. *******
  Non, c'est tout, merci.

d Eh bien, il y a du dentifrice dans la salle de bains . . . et je vais chercher une serviette.
  Say: wait! here's a present for you. *******
  Attends! voici un cadeau pour toi!

e Ah c'est très gentil!
  Say: go on, open it! *******
  Mais vas-y, ouvre-le!

f Ah! une affiche de Charles et Diana! Merci beaucoup!